TAE KWON DO KICKING STRATEGY

by Jun Chong

EMPIRE BOOK/AWP LLC
Los Angeles, CA.

DISCLAIMER

Please note that the author and publisher of this book are NOT RESPONSIBLE in any manner whatsoever for any injury that may result from practicing the techniques and/or following the instructions given within. Since the physical activities described herein may be too strenuous in nature for some readers to engage in safely, it is essential that a physician be consulted prior to training.

Revised Edition published in 2024 by AWP LLC/Empire Books. Copyright (c) 2024 by Jun Chong and AWP LLC/Empire Books.

All rights reserved. No part of this publication may be reproduced or utilized in any form or by any means, electronic or mechanical, including photo- copying, recording, or by any information storage and retrieval system, without prior written permission from AWP LLC/Empire Books.

Revised edition Library of Congress Catalog Number:

ISBN-13: 978-1-949753-70-7

24 23 22 21 20 19 18 17 16 15 14 13 12

Library of Congress Cataloging-in-Publication Data

Tae Kwon Do Kicking Strategy by Jun Chong -- Compiled & Arranged ed. p. cm.

ISBN 978-1-949753-70-7 (pbk. : alk. paper) 1. Martial arts-- philosophy. 3. Large type books. I. Title. GV1114.3.F715

20711161.815'3--dc22

20060187543

Printed in the United States of America.

TABLE OF CONTENTS

ACKNOWLEDGMENTS 7

ABOUT THE AUTHOR 8

PREFACE 10

INTRODUCTION 13

CHAPTER I: LIMBERKING EXERCISES 16

CHAPTER II: USAGE OF THE KNEE IN KICKING 45

CHAPTER III: FRONT KICKS 49

CHAPTER IV: ROUNDHOUSE KICKS 58

CHAPTER V: SIDE KICKS 65

CHAPTER VI: BACK KICKS 72

CHAPTER VII: HOOK KICKS 80

CHAPTER VIII: SPINNING HEEL KICKS 89

CHAPTER IX: DROP KICKS 100

MASTER JUN CHONG: ONE-ON-ONE 104

TAE KWON DO
KICKING STRATEGY

Chong receives his 7th degree in Koju ryu from master Masafumi Suzuki, Seibu Kuan Academy, Kyoto, Japan, 1979. All Japan Budo Federation.

Acknowledgments

My most sincere thanks to Phil Rohlin, who was instrumental in the development of this book, and to Gary Dordick and Peter Luldjuraj for their unselfish contribution of time and effort in demonstrating the following exercises and techniques.

Jun Chong

About the Author

Jun Chong - Tae Kwon Do 9th Degree Black Belt (Kukkiwon)
Hapkido 9th Degree Black Belt (International Hapkido Federation)
Brazilian Jiu Jitsu, 1st Degree Black Belt
Kendo 2nd Degree Black Belt
10th Degree Black Belt Honorary (Pro Tae Kwon Do Federation)

Jun Chong started in the world of martial arts as a shy and frail boy of seven in his native land of Korea. Since then, most of his life has been dedicated to the study, practice and teaching of the Korean arts of Tae Kwon Do and Hapkido. His love for the arts makes the demanding job of instructor an admirable one. He continues to grow and learn new things, trying new approaches and promoting the martial arts to new dimensions inside and outside the dojang. Although he reluctantly accepts the title of "master" from his students, he believes that life is an ongoing learning process, and, at this point, he feels he has much more to accomplish and create. Although an expert in Korean styles, in 1979 he earned his 7th degree black belt in Koju Ryu at the Seibu Kuan Academy in Kyoto, Japan, which is affiliated to the All Japan Budo Federation. Only a handful of instructors—mainly Japanese—have been able to attain this status. After retiring from active tournament competition in the early 70's, he went full time into teaching and presently owns several dojangs centralized in Los Angeles, California.

Chong is also in demand as a martial arts actor and has four films to his credit here and in the Orient. *The Stranger* and *Osaka's Lonely Star*, in addition to several television specials, are among his credits.

When Chong is away from his teaching, he spends his free time practicing kendo (Japanese-style fencing), traditional weapons and gymnastics.

Preface

The strategy of sparring comes after you have worked very hard. To get that far you must first absorb great quantities of discipline, learn to tolerate pain without quitting and master fundamentals to the extent that they become automatic and flow. Strategy comes only after you have learned to really see and then act spontaneously in the utmost harmony with the present moment.

To attain readiness for this state, you enter a new plane of reality. It does not begin happily. The indoctrination is harsh and jarring. There is the austere dojang. Unembellished, there is no modern music, no hype, no womblike comforts. Everything is colorless. White walls, white uniforms hanging in a formless drape about your body, a white belt, no recognition, no definition except that which is imposed in shrill commands from an instructor pushing you to stretch your body, endure the pain, flop your unbalanced physique about the mat out of sync. All this is still totally unintegrated. Your self-esteem is shattered. The thought of going home forms in your mind. It hurts and there's no sympathy because someone is demanding that you give more. Your wife is telling you that it's ridiculous to keep going as you languish in the hot bath soaking in epsom salts. Tomorrow, you stretch through yesterday's pain. Pain is an everyday occurrence. Pain obliterates time, and eats away your confidence. Now the first crisis comes. Everything in you wants to quit.

If you don't quit, then you have accepted pain as a condition of the sport and you have achieved the level of a yellow belt student. As the colored belt winds around your body, you have a slight glimpse of what coordination means. You are ready to spar and you can contort your body into a few kicks and snap your hands through a few blocking motions. Now, you are asked to apply them against an opponent who is moving at you in an unrehearsed but controlled aggression. Everything is out of sync and wooden. You are the victim of a thousand irrelevant movements and you get hurt again and again, because you don't know how to move or think spontaneously. Nothing in your life has prepared you for this. Further pain is accompanied by intimidation. There is no grace in the feeble movements you execute across the mat.

Your movement is without grace. Your feeble thrusts, abortive charges, hopeless stabbing and chopping movements register across your mind in an ineffective blur. You move forward into an impression of overwhelming vulnerability as you come into your opponent's range. You become aware of your distance and your risks when you close the space. You see what you can walk into if your aggressiveness leads you into a cleverly defended opposition. Perhaps you become aware of a new humility, a sense that there is more to this than a simple application of the mechanical. Even memorization doesn't help. The techniques you learned at school dissolve in the face of this new reality. Something here transcends the mechanical. You are reaching a new stage of awareness that fixes you to the present moment like never before. There is no point of reference for this moment. You have never experienced it before.

Sparring in its refined and exalted stages quiets the mind and focuses its awareness into a total time vacuum. Imagine all your nerve endings and mental perceptions welded to the flickering impressions registered by your eyeball. There are no other thoughts, no other reactions, no other reality but the kaleidoscope impressions recorded in perpetual motion on your retina. No past or future, just an ever-shifting present in the realm of perception. This is the world of sparring. Strategy takes shape in this domain of instantaneous perception. When you have crossed into this quicksilver reality you can apply strategy to your sparring.

Strategy is the application of intelligence to this very process of the instantaneous. It not only changes the way you spar, but transforms the way you live and dissolves your mind into the plane of immediacy. This book deals with this strategy, the quintessence of what it means to be a martial artist. Master it and you have mastered yourself and brought your mind into permanent equilibrium.

Phillip Rohlin, Tae Kwon Do first dan black belt, Jun Chong's student

Introduction

To the uninitiated, at first glance what may seem like a wild exchange of kicks and punches is called free style sparring. In reality, it involves myriad details, a melange of the subtle and intricate interplay of several factors including physical ability, reaction time, fighting experience, type of training, and a "sixth" sense to anticipate the opponent's movements. Because of the concentration it requires, sparring is one of the most exciting and productive exercises in the martial arts to blend the mind and body. Good kicking ability, exclusively, does not ensure success in a match. A fighter who knows when to attack, when to retreat and when to counterattack undoubtedly has the upper-hand.

Strategy applies to the use of techniques in direct relation to the circumstances which can only be assessed by the mind. Superior sparring involves the contenders who execute a technique in the most effective way at the precise fraction of the second and make it work. Anything other than that is wasted motion and energy. When a match is over, the worse fighter is usually more tired from wasting too much energy, being too tense, or perhaps lacking breath control. Most failures stem from two causes: Not watching the opponent in a constructive way, and lacking continuity of techniques due to poor concentration and ability.

Not many fighters in the martial arts make the best of kicking. They limit themselves to two or three basic kicks out of habit or fear of trying something "too risky". Being a Tae Kwon Do stylist, myself, I favor the use of the legs. There is actually an arsenal of kicks that give very good results, including a few of the fancier kind. The idea is to be versatile and surprise your opponent once in a while. Needless to say, good physical condition is necessary because the attacks and counterattacks must be executed crisply and with balance. For that reason, this book may appeal especially to the intermediate and advanced student who has mastered the basic mechanics of kicking.

To decide what techniques to use with success, you may consider the following points:
1. Are you facing the same or opposite way [in relation to your opponent]?
2. Is he taller or shorter? Does he have long or short reach?
3. Does he always kick with the same leg? Does he have a favorite technique or combination?

4. In his attitude, is he the type who backs away dodging blows or does he stand fast and block without moving very much out of your way?
5. Do you detect a *kamikaze* attitude or more of a defensive one? (The *kamikaze* character will charge at you with all he's got, hoping something will connect. On the other hand, the defensive type sits back and waits for you to make the first mistake and then springs into action.)
6. Are his hands up, protecting his head? Does he protect his rib cage? Look for openings, take advantage of his negligence, while you keep up your own guard.

It doesn't take long to notice and quickly study your opponent's weak and strong points by keeping steady eye contact with him. Of course, how smart a fighter you become depends greatly on your natural ability to make quick judgements. There are, however, a few things you can do to help your sparring besides watching your opponent:

1. Be light on your feet, shifting your weight to the balls of the feet instead of standing flat-footed.
2. Snap kicks in and out quickly, recoiling the leg fully to avoid being grabbed or trapped.
3. Learn to judge distances for kicking as well as punching. Being too close or too far may be the only flaw in an otherwise perfect technique.
4. Don't spend all your energy during the first few moments of a match. Don't show your entire repertoire in the first half of the fight.
5. Like a good chess player, never make a move that does not have a purpose.

Perhaps, all this advice may sound a bit too calculating and too controlled, but as I said before, physical ability alone is not enough to spar with finesse. Sparring is fun. Not only is it a tremendous test of stamina, but it keeps your mind alert, tuned and trained to act under stress.

The combinations for attacks and counterattacks given in the following chapters are only guidelines. You can create your own combinations, fakes and set-ups as long as you take your partner into account. Remember, sparring is not a solo sport. While you may be watching your opponent, he is also watching you.

THE CONTROL FACTOR.

Let's make it perfectly clear that sparring is not to be compared or confused with street fighting strategy. There is a difference between self-defense fighting and sparring. I don't consider them in the same category. The techniques described here are for those who truly love the art of sparring per se, incorporating a martial arts spirit within a martial art environment. This may sound a bit esoteric, and it just may be, but hopefully, only those trained in the martial arts can execute these feats. Sparring is treated here like a sport and an exercise of matching the physical and mental abilities of two partners. It is not a life and death encounter.

A trained and confident fighter does not have to hurt his opponent in order to show his superiority. He knows how much power must be released on impact with undeniable target accuracy. He does not draw blood. I realize that accidents occur; it comes with the territory, but there is no need to hurt someone to prove who is better.

I have never forgotten a young black belt I sparred with in my days of high school competition. What impressed me the most about him was his uncanny ability to anticipate my intentions. Because of this, he was always ready to counter-attack. On the other hand, I was never aware of his swift techniques coming at me. It was like suddenly seeing a foot or fist at my face, barely grazing my cheek or nose. It never had force that would have made it deadly. I was, of course, frustrated because I could not outwit him. I finally realized, however, that I had a long way to go before I could equal his poise, speed and control. This experience served to raise the standards I had set for myself as a martial artist. Finally, I had seen with my own eyes the difference between an ego-loaded fighter and a noble one. Full power behind those blows, at that time, would have been detrimental had I been a real enemy.

The first consideration for the proper harnessing of power is to prevent injuries that could prove painfully disabling or even fatal to your partner (who, we must always remember, is not our enemy.) Although light contact is necessary and even recommended, sparring is not a duel or a contest of the hardest hitter. An injured party wastes time, misses training and even, in some cases, may abandon practice altogether. If you have a need to unleash all that pent up energy inside, use a punching bag instead. Gracefulness and control are what separate the ordinary slugger and the martial artist.

CHAPTER 1
Limbering Exercises

Flexibility and strength go hand in hand for better kicking results. The following exercises are excellent to improve the muscle tone and flexibility of the legs, hips and back. Add them to any warmup routine you already have before starting your workout.

Waist Bend

1) Initial position: Stand with your feet apart and your hands on your waist.

2) Lean the upper part of your body forward. Your palms rest on the floor.

3) Continue by extending the arms under and behind you as far as you can.

4) With your hands on your waist, stretch all the way back in an arch. Repeat eight times, starting from the initial position.

Thigh Stretch

From the waist bend initial position, bend the knees almost to a sitting position. Keep the upper body straight and aligned with the hips. Hold to the count of ten. Slowly return to the initial position.

Waist Turn

1) From the waist bend initial position (on page 6), grab the left ankle with both hands and bend along the left leg as far down as you can. Hold to the count of ten.

2) Repeat on the other side.

3) Grab both ankles and pull yourself down until the backs of your legs are fully stretched. Hold to the count of ten. Return to the waist bend initial position and repeat.

Front Stance Stretch

1) Assume this position. Exagerate the position of the back leg until the front thigh is fully stretched. Keep your back straight. Hold to the count of ten. Repeat with each leg at least twice.

2) Then, with your hands on your hips, bend forward as far as far as you can. Hold to the count of ten. Repeat with each leg.

Back Stance Stretch

1) Assume this position. Rest your weight on the right leg, knee bent, foot flat on floor. Extend the other leg sideways. Hold to the count of ten.

2) Hold ankles and bend to touch outstretched leg with your forehead. Hold to the count of ten. Repeat with the other leg.

Sitting Back Stretch

1) Initial position: Sit with legs out and together, toes up, hands on waist.

2) Lean forward and hold feet or ankles.

3) Slowly lower your chest to your knees, or as far as you can go.

4) Return to the initial position. Lean backwards and slowly raise your legs. Keep your knees straight. (continued on next page)

Sitting Back Stretch

5) Continue to bring the legs up and over your head until your toes touch the floor. Hold to the count of ten.

6) Walk your toes toward your head as you slightly lower your hips.

7) Lock hands together over ankles and hold legs straight to the count of ten. Slowly lower your legs.

8) Return to the initial position and repeat.

Sitting Back Stretch

9) From the initial position, bring the right foot toward you and rest the ankle on your left thigh.

10) Embrace the stretched leg and pull yourself toward the knee.

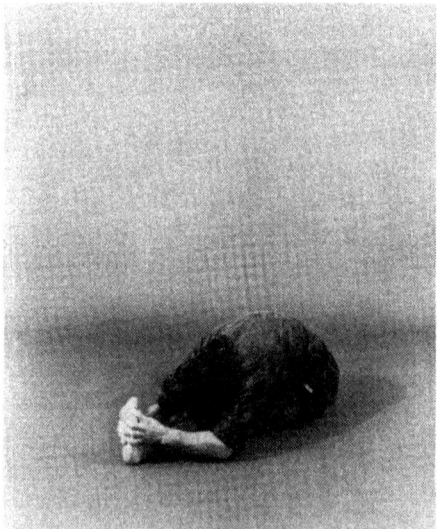

11) For additional stretching, hold the foot instead of the calf. Count to ten. Repeat with the other leg.

Hamstring Stretch

1) Initial position: Stand straight with your feet together and your arms at your side.

2) Grab your ankles.

3) Side view. Slowly move yourself down.

4) Lock your arms behind the calves and attempt to bring the chest to the knees. Hold to the count of ten. Return to the initial position and repeat.

Splits

1) Initial position: Crouch with legs spread in a wide "V" formation.

2) Extend legs sideways and lean forward. Support your weight with your hands. Slowly rock back and forth several times, then hold to the count of ten.

3) Gradually bring your groin to the floor. Point your toes forward. Relax. Don't fight the stretch; let yourself go until you've given all you have to give. Don't tense yourself; this causes the muscles to contract.

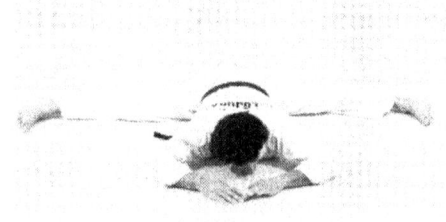

4) Lean forward until your forehead touches the floor. Hold to the count of ten. Return to the initial position. (continued on next page)

Splits

1) From the initial position, shown on page 15, turn your body and hips to the left and lower yourself into a side split. Hold to the count of ten.

2) Lean forward along the left leg. Hold to the count of ten.

3) Slowly return to the upright side split and arch your back as much as possible. Hold to the count of ten. Return to the initial position and repeat with the other leg.

Waist Stretch

1) Bend from the waist along the inside of the left leg. Grab your ankle with your right hand. Hold to the count of ten.

2) Repeat on the other leg.

Inner Thigh Stretch

1) Kneel, and lean on your elbows. Spread the thighs as wide as possible. Slowly rock the pelvis back and forth several times, then slightly push back. Hold to the count of ten.

2) Without moving your knees, bring your upper body up and arch your back. Hold to the count of ten.

3) Lean backwards until your back rests on the floor. Hold to the count of ten.

Bridge

1) Lie on your back. Bring your knees up and place feet flat on floor. Bend your elbows and turn your hands in by the shoulders.

2) Exert pressure on your hands and feet to lift your pelvis and back off the floor as high as possible. Your arms should be locked. Hold to the count of ten, and lower yourself to the floor. Repeat five times.

Bow

1) From a kneeling position, grab your heels with your hands.

2) Hold your heels and push your hips forward. Hold to the count of ten.

The following exercises can be done using a bar or rail, they can also be done with a partner. Take turns doing these stretching exercises. Working with a partner makes the exercises more interesting and helps you to concentrate.

Front Kick Stretch

1) Place your left foot on your partner's right shoulder (or on the bar).

2) Bend forward to your knee. Keep your legs straight. Hold to the count of ten.

Side Kick Stretch

1) Place left foot on your partner's shoulder (or on the bar). Turn your hips to the right into a simulated side kick. Your standing foot should now face away from your partner.

2) Have your partner slowly walk away from you one or two steps until you reach your maximum stretch. Or if you are using a bar, slowly walk away from it. Remember to point the heel up. Hold to the count of ten.

Back Kick Stretch

1) With your left foot on your partner's shoulder (or on the bar), face away from your partner. Set your position for a back kick with the knee locked.

2) Lean forward towards the floor. Hold to the count of ten. At this point, switch legs and start with the front kick stretch again.

Partner Stretch Kick

1) Initial position: Hold the bar (or partner). Put your right foot slightly forward.

2) Bring the right leg to a side kick position and hold to the count of ten. Slowly lower the leg. Return to the initial position.

3) After you slowly lower the leg, swing the right leg as high as possible. Remember to turn the hips inward and downward. Repeat ten times.

Partner Stretch Kick

1) From the same initial position as on page 24, look over your shoulder and swing the leg out behind you. Aim the kick directly behind you this time, not sideways. Repeat ten times.

2) From the initial position, bring the leg halfway up to a fully stretched position, and hold to the count of ten. Slowly lower the leg, and repeat with the opposite leg.

Half Circle Stretch Kick

1) Initial position: Hold the bar (or partner) with the feet slightly apart, then slide the right foot next to the left, with the knee flexed as shown.

2) Execute a high hook kick . . .

3) Swinging the foot up to twelve o'clock . . .

Half Circle Stretch Kick

4) Around to nine o' clock . . .

5) Landing the foot behind you after having brought the foot in a complete circle.

Full Circle Stretch Kick

1) Initial position: Hold the bar (or partner) with your right foot in front of your left, as shown.

2) Begin by swinging the right leg sideways . . .

3) Around to twelve o'clock . . .

Full Circle Stretch Kick

4) Past twelve o'clock . . .

5) Until you have made a full circle behind yourself.

6) Land on the opposite side, as in a spinning heel kick. Be careful not to drop the leg too soon. Repeat ten times with each leg.

Solo Stretch Kick

1) Initial position: Natural front stance.

2) Swing the rear leg, with knee locked, to touch your shoulder. Repeat seven times.

3) From the same initial position, swing the leg up and across your chest to touch the shoulder opposite your kicking leg.

Solo Stretch Kick

1) Assume the natural front stance, the initial position.

2) Swing the back leg out to the side, outside your shoulder. Repeat seven times with each leg.

Crescent Kicks

1) Initial position: Natural front stance.

2) Keep the knee straight. Swing the back leg forward into a wide circle that starts from the center of your body.

3) The apex of the swing, at twelve o'clock.

Crescent Kicks

4) Around to ten o'clock.

5) Repeat this circular swing seven times. Then repeat the circle moving in the opposite direction seven times. Repeat with the other leg an equal number of times.

CHAPTER 2
Usage of the Knee in Kicking

    While it is true that turning the hips account for a more powerful and penetrating thrust, the knee also plays an important part in the execution of kicks. Setting the knee in the right position accounts for speed, perfect aiming and snap. In general, the higher the knee is raised, the higher the kick, and vice-versa. Because the foot, connected in a straight line by the shin to the knee joint, can never be aimed higher or lower than the level the knee is cocked. "Coiling" the leg, as it is also called, gives you more opportunity for faking or executing two or three kicks in succession with the same foot. For example, a hook kick and a roundhouse kick naturally follow each other for a good combination. Or, a front kick followed by a side kick is also effective. The combinations are possible only by bringing the knee back and making it ready to be snapped out again.

Knee Tucking Exercises

1) Initial Position: Natural front stance.

2) Bring your back leg up so that the knee touches your chest. Hold the raised leg and keep the foot parallel to the floor. Hold to the count of seven.

3) Snap the leg into a front kick, then recoil the knee to your chest. Return to the initial position. Repeat five times with each leg.

Knee Tucking Exercises

1) From a natural stance, pivot on the ball of the front foot and set the back leg for a roundhouse kick.

2) Set the knee high and sideways. Turn the upper body and hips prior to kicking. Hold the ankle to the count of seven.

3) Extend the kick, then recoil to the initial position, a natural front stance. Repeat five times with each leg.

Knee Tucking Exercises

1) Assume the initial position, a natural front stance.

2) Pivot on the ball of the front foot. Bring the back leg to chest level. Hold to the count of seven.

3) Extend the raised leg into a side kick. Turn the hips in and down. Pull the leg back, bring the knee to the chest. Return to the initial position. Repeat five times with each leg.

CHAPTER 3
Front Kicks

Attacking Techniques

Using a standing front kick:

1) Situation: Partners face the same side.

2) Fake a high reverse punch.

3) Immediately follow with a high front kick.

4) Deliver the kick to the face.

Attacking Techniques

Using jumping front kicks:

1) Situation: Partners face the same side.

2) Bring up the rear leg and fake a set-up for a front kick.

3) Instead, execute a jumping front kick.

4) With your rear leg, deliver the kick to the face.

Attacking Techniques

1) Situation: Partners face opposite sides.

2) Sweep or "hook" your partner's front leg. It isn't necessary to bring him down, but merely upset his balance and concentration.

3) Follow the sweep with a jumping front kick.

4) Deliver the kick to the face.

Counterattacks for Roundhouse Kicks

Using a standing front kick:

1) Situation: Partners face the same side.

2) Slide back. At the same time, block the kick with a knife hand.

3) Bring your elbows to your sides and hands to face level to cover a possible counterpunch.
(continued on next page)

Counterattacks for Roundhouse Kicks

4) Quickly snap a front kick to the face or chest.

5) If your partner avoids the previous kick, immediately recoil the leg. Step in at a forty-five degree angle and deliver a reverse punch to the midsection.

Counterattacks for Roundhouse Kicks

Using a jumping front kick:

1) Situation: Partners face the same side.

2) Move back slightly, almost to a cat stance.

3) At the same time, use an inside block.

Counterattacks for Roundhouse Kicks

4) Without taking an extra step, jump. Tuck your knees as high as possible.

5) Deliver a front kick at face level.

HINTS FOR A BETTER FRONT KICK

Thrust your hips forward as you kick, driving the leg deep to make contact with the ball of the foot, not the toes. If fanning the toes is difficult, practice bending them against the floor.

CHAPTER 4
Roundhouse Kicks

Attacking Techniques

Using a sliding roundhouse kick:

1) Situation: Partners face the same side.

2) Jab and slide the rear leg forward.

3) As your partner pulls away from the jab, begin a roundhouse kick.

4) Deliver the kick to the side of the head.

Attacking Techniques

Using a jumping roundhouse kick:

1) Situation: Partners face opposite sides.

2) Fake a sweep with the rear leg.

3) Use the momentum of the sweep to execute a jumping roundhouse kick at face level.

4) Deliver the kick to the side of the head.

Counterattacks for Side and Front Kicks

Using a spinning roundhouse kick against a side kick:

1) Situation: Partners face the same side.

2) As soon as your partner moves into a side kick, step back. Your elbow is ready to block.

3) Delfect the kick outward with your elbow.

Counterattacks for Side and Front Kicks

4) At the same time, throw a spinning roundhouse kick.

5) Deliver the kick to the open side of your partner's face.

Counterattacks for Side and Front Kicks

Jumping roundhouse after a front kick:

1) Situation: Partners face the same side.

2) Slide back into cat stance. Turn your body away from the kick and block at the same time.

3) Immediately follow up with a jumping roundhouse kick.

4) Deliver the kick to the face.

HINTS FOR BETTER ROUNDHOUSE KICKS

As for sparring, the striking part of the foot is usually the instep. To ensure penetration, imagine a point beyond the target. This applies to all kicks. The sharp turning of the hips is vital for the success of this kick which is frequently used in sparring. Note: When we say penetration, we do not mean it literally in the physical sense, in this case, we apply this term to the trajectory of the kick itself.

CHAPTER 5
Side Kicks

Attacking Techniques

Using a sliding side kick:

1) Situation: Partners face the same side.

2) Jab to the face, and slide sideways and over with the rear leg.

3) The jab is blocked.

4) Immediately follow with a side kick to the exposed side.

Attacking Techniques

Using a jumping side kick:

1) Situation: Partners face opposite sides.

2) Fake a deep, low punch.

3) Quickly switch and fake a punch to the face. Note how close the fakes appear; it is important to draw from your partner a commitment to block them. (continued on next page)

Attacking Techniques

4) Immediately, as the second punch is blocked, execute a jumping side kick.

5) Deliver the kick to the head.

Counterattacks for Side and Front Kicks

Standing side kick after a front kick:

1) Situation: Partners face the same side.

2) As your partner's knee is set for a front kick (or he turns his body toward you), raise your front knee to chest level.

3) Lunge forward and snap a side kick to the jaw. Lean away from his kick. Note: This counterattack must happen with split second timing, the instant you see the set-up for the front kick. And to avoid his kick's line of fire, keep your body facing him at a forty-five degree angle.

Counterattacks for Side and Front Kicks

Jumping side kick after a sliding side kick:

1) Situation: Partners face opposite sides.

2) As your partner slides sideways toward you, bring your front leg back and across the rear foot. Keep your distance.

3) At the same time, block and deflect the kick to the side.

4) Follow with a jumping kick.

Counterattacks for Side and Front Kicks

5) Deliver the kick to the side of the head.

HINTS FOR BETTER SIDE KICKS

The striking area is the blade of the foot. Executed correctly, side kicks are beautiful and deadly. Best of all, they lend themselves to many situations. Nothing is more important than pivoting the hips and foot (the standing foot) as the kick is delivered.

CHAPTER 6
Back Kicks

Attacking Techniques

Using a standing back kick:

1) Situation: Partners face the same side.

2) Fake a deep reverse punch.

3) At the same time, turn around by stepping over your pivoting front foot.

Attacking Techniques

4) Look over your shoulder.

5) When your partner is on target, snap a medium level back kick.

6) Deliver the kick to the midsection.

Attacking Techniques

Using a jumping back kick:

1) Situation: Partners face the same side.

2) Jab with hand closest to opponent.

3) Follow with a reverse punch.

Attacking Techniques

4) With the reverse punch, simultaneously fake a set-up for a roundhouse kick.

5) Instead, jump off the standing leg and pivot in the opposite direction. Execute a standing back kick. Deliver the kick to the face or upper body.

Counterattacks for Roundhouse Kicks

1) Situation: Partners face the same side.

2) Slide back (but not too far away). Simultaneously block the kick with an inside block.

3) Pivot away from the kick. Turn your head and look over your shoulder.

4) Immediately deliver a back kick to either the face, chest, or midsection.

Counterattacks for Roundhouse Kicks

Jumping back kick after a roundhouse kick:

1) Situation: Partners face opposite sides.

2) As your opponent attempts a low roundhouse kick aimed at the midsection, jam it by bringing up your rear knee sideways.

3) As your knee is raised, jump off the standing leg. Pivot in mid air for a jumping back kick.

4) Although Chong can execute this kick at face level, the chest and midsection are acceptable targets.

HINTS FOR A BETTER BACK KICK

It is easy to miss your target with a back kick if the leg strays sideways. Your back should face the opponent completely, then snap the kick directly behind you, the heel must point at the target.

CHAPTER 7
Hook Kick

Attacking Techniques

Using a standing hook kick:

1) Partners face the same side.

2) Fake a set-up for a side kick.

3) Instead, fake a low side kick to your opponent's knee.

Attacking Techniques

4) Immediately recock your leg and set up for another side kick.

5) Instead, lunge forward towards your opponent.

6) Throw a hook kick aimed at the face.

Attacking Techniques

Using a jumping hook kick:

1) Situation: Partners face opposite sides.

2) Fake a low reverse punch, which can easily be blocked.

3) Follow with a jab to the face. Bring both feet together. Keep your knees slightly flexed.

Attacking Techniques

4) Immediately after the jab is blocked, jump. Keep your knees tucked up.

5) Execute a jumping hook kick.

6) Deliver the kick to the face.

Counterattacks for Side and Front Kicks

Using a standing hook kick after a front kick:

1) Situation: Partners face opposite sides.

2) As your opponent attempts to throw a front kick, raise your knee to cover your upper body. Fake a set-up for a side kick.

3) Avoid his kick by slightly pivoting your body. Follow through with a hook kick.

4) Deliver the kick to the face.

Counterattacks for Side and Front Kicks

Jumping hook kick after a side kick:

1) Situation: Partners face the same side.

2) Slide back to a cat stance.

3) Deflect your opponent's kick to the side.

4) Immediately follow with a jumping hook kick. (continued on next page)

Counterattacks for Side and Front Kicks

5) Execute the jumping hook kick at face level.

6) Target the kick for your opponent's head.

HINTS FOR A BETTER HOOK KICK

Usually the hook kick is aimed at the head and is derived directly from the side kick, but adding the "hook." The key to these kicks is a quick snap. Hook kicks are usually used after a faking technique. Less experienced fighters swing their hook kicks in a wide circle and are easily blocked. Snap it in as you would a side kick, executing the "hook" at the moment of impact.

CHAPTER 8
Spinning Heel Kick

Counterattacks for Roundhouse and Back Kicks

4) Bring the back leg straight up.

5) Remember: Your kicking leg should touch your shoulder; a low drop kick has no effect.

6) Bring the kick down on either the face or chest.

Counterattacks for Roundhouse and Back Kicks

After a back kick:

1) Partners face opposite sides.

2) Slide back to avoid the kick.

3) As you slide, use a low block to deflect the kick to the side. This puts your opponent in position for your next set up.

Counterattacks for Roundhouse and Back Kicks

4) Jump, and execute a drop kick.

5) Raise your kicking leg as high as possible.

6) Bring the kick down on your opponent's shoulder or head.

HINTS FOR A BETTER DROP KICK

Although they are not too popular in the United States, drop kicks are widely used in Korea by tae kwon do competitors. While other kicks need some distance in order to be effective, the drop kick is used when the opponent is in close range. Flexibility is the key to this technique, lunging forward with the hips for reach. Power is also an important requirement.

Attacking Techniques

1) Partners face the same side.

2) Lead with a fake high punch.

3) Sweep your opponent's front leg to upset his balance.

Attacking Techniques

4) Turn until your back faces your opponent.

5) Then, use the turn's momentum, and whip the other leg into a spinning heel kick.

6) Aim the kick at face level.

Counterattacks for Front and Roundhouse Kicks:

Spinning heel after a roundhouse kick:

1) Situation: Partners face the same side.

2) Block the roundhouse kick with a knife hand.

3) Begin a full circle turn away from the kick. Look over your shoulder.

Counterattacks for Front and Roundhouse Kicks

4) When your body is turned, begin to raise your front leg.

5) Continue turning and execute a spinning heel kick.

6) Aim the kick at your opponent's face.

Counterattacks for Front and Roundhouse Kicks

Jump spinning heel after a front kick:

1) Situation: Partners face the same side.

2) As your opponent delivers a front kick, jump sideways to avoid it. Tuck your legs up.

3) Turn in mid-air and execute a spinning heel kick.

4) Deliver the kick to your opponent's face.

HINTS FOR A BETTER SPINNING HEEL KICK

Speed and balance are of prime importance in the success of this kick. Its peak or point of impact is directly behind you, so avoid dropping the foot too low while it travels in a wide circle. For light sparring, the sole of the foot may also be used as the striking area.

CHAPTER 9
Drop Kicks

Attacking Techniques

Using a standing drop kick:

1) Situation: Partners face opposite sides.

2) Sweep your opponent's front leg. This will upset his balance. There's no need to bring him down.

3) With your other leg, immediately follow with a drop kick. Remember: your kicking leg should touch your shoulder; a low drop kick will have no effect.

4) Drop the kick on your opponent's face or chest.

Attacking Techniques

Using a jumping drop kick:

1) Situation: Partners face the same side.

2) Fake a low reverse side kick to the opponent's knee.

3) Jump, and bring the other leg as high as possible.

4) Land the drop kick to the side of the neck or head.

Counterattacks for Roundhouse and Back Kicks

Drop kick after a spinning roundhouse:

1) Situation: Partners face the same side.

2) Deflect the roundhouse kick with an outside block, and turn your body at a forty-five degree angle to get out of range.

3) With hips thrust forward, execute a drop kick with the back leg.

MASTER JUN CHONG: ONE ON ONE

What prompted you to get involved in martial arts?

I wanted to learn how to defend myself from the big guys. I was always small as a kid and even now I'm only 5'6" tall. I was raised by my mother, without a father to take care of me. I had no family support outside of my mother. She encouraged me to take martial arts. The training was very hard and I was shy and had a weak mind at first. When I was ten years old, I got injured: my arm was cracked from a side kick. So I quit for three or four months. My mother was very supportive. I was scared by the injury, but she encouraged me to continue. She set up private lessons two times a week, for several years. Through this individualized instruction, I got physically stronger and also developed a stronger self-image and character.

At that time there were no international federations of any kind. When I trained, all the different Kwans were active. My master was from Song Moo Kwan Master Kim II Sung. My mother, who was a single parent, wanted me to know how to protect myself because I was an only child. During that particular time, right after the Korean War, things could get a little rough. Many people did not have money and there were some hard times in Korea. At first, I was a bit hesitant, but I needed some discipline. I may have been a little bit scared too, but that may have stemmed from a lack of confidence. Initially, I went five days per week. Of course when my arm was broken I got scared and didn't want to train anymore. I thought the sport was too rough.

Eventually, my skill and confidence grew. My teacher taught me how to spar and convinced me to compete. He gave me confidence in everyday life, not just in martial arts. Even today, I use his methods when I teach. At the time we did non-contact sparring, so this really helped my coordination, balance, timing, speed, and strategy. This also enabled me to use more techniques because it was non-contact. If you go with contact, you have to limit your techniques. We used to train outside in the yard, even during the winter. We used to practice in the rain and snow for hours. I still remember those types of things.

Was it difficult to practice in such bad weather?

Well, we did not wear shoes so it was pretty slippery and cold. However, once we got going and got sweaty, the cold did not bother us. When it snowed hard, sometimes it was hard to focus, at least at first. Eventually, my focus improved. In fact, training in the snow enabled me to strengthen my focus and concentration skills. If I could focus during that, I was confident that I could focus through anything ▨ including a fight. Training during the rain made the practices slippery and uncomfortable because water splashed into my face, but it was fun. We also hung a heavy bag from a tree and threw kicks for 30 to 40 minutes almost every practice. Eventually, those trees started to die.

After several years, Mr. Cho went into military, and I never saw him after that. I did learn to not go into the snow to practice the martial arts (laughing). Seriously, I think it's important for beginners to start with non-contact sparring. This enables them to become very natural in their techniques once they do contact sparring. I also learned that even when you are angry, you should not hurt your opponent. The purpose of the martial arts is to provide balance and control.

Did you ultimately get back into formal training?

Yes. There was a taekwondo team at our school, and I trained almost eight hours per day. I would get up at 6 a.m. and do a two-hour workout, I'd do an hour at lunch, more time after school, and then I would train from 6 p.m. to 9 p.m. in the dojang (training hall). I'd finally get home about 10:30 p.m. Sometimes, I would think about how to fight on the way home on the bus and other times I'd just fall asleep because I'd be so tired. I had six years of that routine.

Do you have an orientation toward the traditional aspects of martial arts?

I think traditional is the right way to teach. In high school in Korea, I got into tournament competition. They were not like tournaments today. In those days, tournaments were very physical and there were no limitations on techniques. You could have many techniques, like punching to the face, sweeps, and grabs. Today, there are many rules. I think martial arts have to allow more varied ways of defense and use every possible situation of a real fight. I think this is very

important and should not be limited. In the 1970's tournaments, even though they allowed more techniques, they were controlled in other ways. Tournaments had respect and a sense of beauty. Nowadays, competitors wear no uniforms, carry a radio, do not bow, and show no respect. It is foolish to make a tournament like that. I think students should avoid these kinds of tournaments. I'm afraid my students will go and learn bad attitudes! In my studio, we teach how to respect. There are a lot of big names in tournaments and the Olympics, but in the long run this is limited. They may kick well, but they are leaving out most everything else which is important to the martial arts.

Did you always want to come to the United States?

Not really. Actually, I was going to go into the military. Later, however, I had a chance to come to America, which is what I did. After high school, in 1966, an American family adopted me. I was 18, but they reduced my age for the adoption to 15. I moved with them to Olympia, Washington. My mother approached them because she felt there was no future in Korea. She worked on a United States military base and met a man and wife who did not have kids. She recommended that they adopt me. To be honest, at first I didn't like it. After I thought about it, though, I thought it might be a good chance to make a living in America. At that time, Korea was a poor country and there were times when we had to fight for food. These people, Mr. and Mrs. Graf, were very nice people.

Los Angeles is a big place for a young man on his own.

After graduating from high school and coming to the United States, I studied with hapkido founder Sea Oh Choi for four years. He taught me the real knowledge of the martial arts. Hapkido is pure knowledge: knowledge of throwing techniques, kicking techniques, and punching techniques. During those four years I learned from him spiritually, too. I also looked for a taekwondo school that needed an instructor. I met Mr. Choi in Gardena, California and I asked him for a job. That was in 1968, and I stayed with him until 1972. I stayed in the studio and slept there and cleaned the school. I tried to go to college but it didn't work out so I did martial arts full-time. Then I opened my own school in Rosemead, California in 1972. Three years later I bought Chuck Norris' school on Wilshire Boulevard in Los Angeles. I had 200 students within two years and 400 within four years. I still have my school on Wilshire Boulevard in Beverly Hills, and we offer 11 classes per day, and are open seven days a week. I think that one of the reasons we're successful is that I give hard martial arts to my students. They accept that and appreciate it.

What do you mean by "hard" martial arts?

The students are very focused and there is plenty of strong, physical work. There may not always be contact, but there is lots of kicking and punching combinations, lots of time devoted to practicing techniques, and the action is non-stop. I truly believe that the only formula for success is hard work. I think it also helps that we blend taekwondo and hapkido. With taekwondo, the students get a lot of kicking and punching ▢ they sweat a lot and spar a lot. On the other hand, hapkido is calm with its hand grabs, takedowns, and joint locks. These two arts give students a balance in class, and that is how I teach. After they are sweating from the kicking and punching, we stop and do some hapkido movements. Once they've had a chance to cool down while doing hapkido movements, we start with some hard kicks. The balance is good for the class. I think it's also because we provide flexible hours. We have many professionals who train here and time is a concern therefore we have flexible hours.

You have trained in many other systems. Why?

I just want to know what tai chi was, what aikido was, and what shotokan was. I wondered what the difference was between aikido and hapkido, and so I found out for myself instead of asking someone. Aikido is more graceful and more precise with each lock. Hapkido is more powerful and more physical. It's graceful too, but it has more power. Tai chi has very soft power. I always get stiff after tai chi workouts because there is no training quite like it. In taekwondo, we stretch ourselves to our utmost physical limits and totally put ourselves mentally and physically into it. Tai chi, on the other hand, is very slow. Dan Lee always says how tai chi is different from taekwondo. Of course they are different ⬚ but that doesn't mean one is good and one is bad. Everybody is different. For some people, tight is good and for others tight is bad. So for some people taekwondo is good and for others it is not. All styles are different and none is the best for everybody.

What is your teaching methodology?

I think the master must have strong discipline to be at the school every day. No matter how many students come, I teach ⬚ even if it is only one student. I give sincere teaching, with the philosophy that one student will bring ten students later. When beginners first walk-in, I make it very loose, very relaxed. I teach them a relaxed meditation for five minutes, Then I teach yoga stretches and breathing, combined with taekwondo stretches for about 15 minutes. Next we do punching techniques, somewhat like shotokan punches, and we perform a routine of blocks. Then we start kicking stretch kicks and kicks. After a little more stretching, we do hyungs or forms.

People continually want to learn. I am always learning. My students are the same way. So I teach what I know and I teach what I learn. This is what it means to be a master: to keep learning and stay ahead of your students, bringing new things for them to learn! Many people limit themselves. I feel no one martial art is best. I've become an American taekwondo martial arts school. Although I teach one traditional style, I have brought in many other things. We teach meditation. We also teach the meaning of techniques. Like when you throw a kick, you must understand why. Perhaps we show a defensive position. There is a different spiritual involvement when you think about what you are doing. Besides teaching many techniques, the most important point is that I am disciplined. I know many

great instructors, but they are not disciplined enough. I workout every day and discipline is the most important principle of all. The instructor must be more strongly disciplined than the students. Then everybody will follow the instructor.

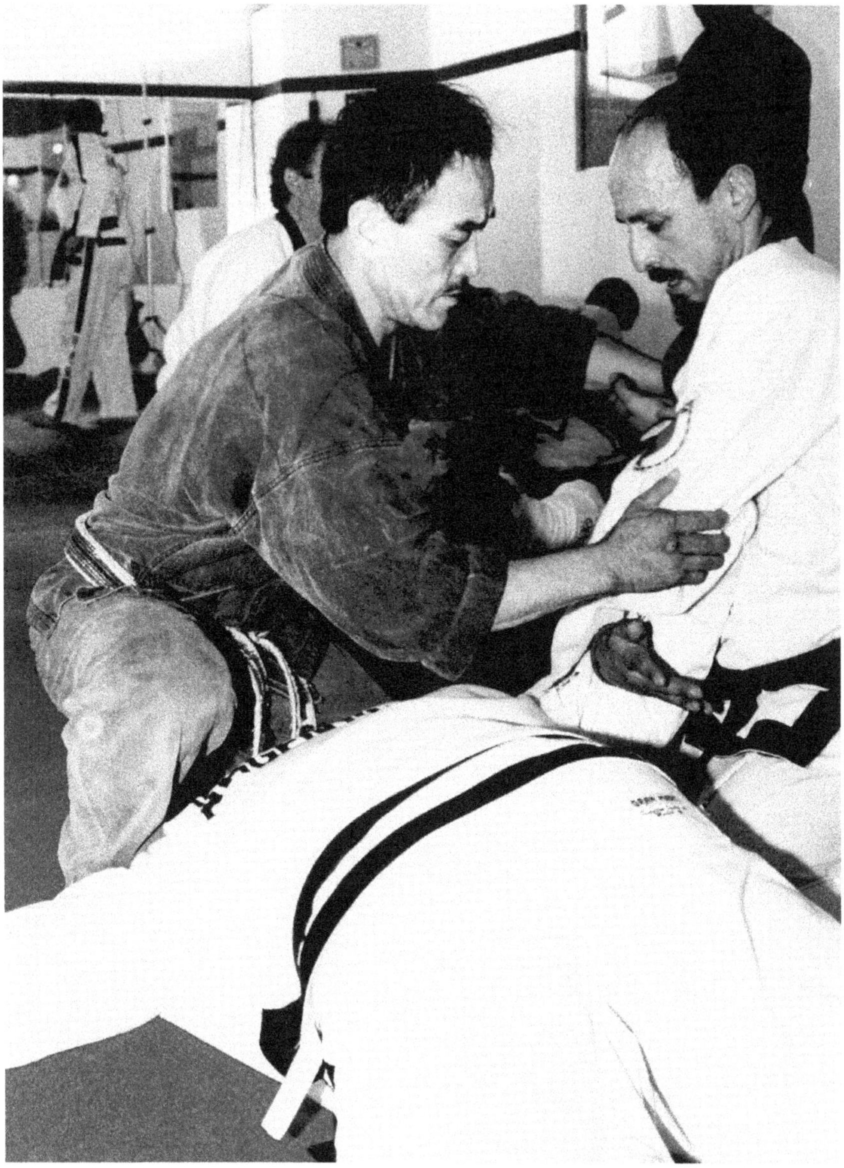

Which hyungs do you teach?

We do Palgwe hyungs, though I changed them a little. The traditional Palgwes were designed by old instructors and they are a little stiff. They look more complicated to learn, but they are more challenging that way. Then I teach how to fall. The traditional taekwondo doesn't usually teach how to fall. We also teach self-defense against grabs ⊠ how to deal with somebody who grabs the neck, or from behind, et cetera. Students love the self-defense training because it is very practical. Finally, we teach jumping kicks and one-on-one sparring, but no-contact sparring at this level. After the first year, I teach more advanced methods of kicking and punching. It's organized with the same routine, but has more advanced techniques. At the black belt level, I teach boxing. All of my black belts know how to box, which is combined with our kicks. But kickboxing can be sloppy. In taekwondo, punching and kicking is more focused, with many different varieties of punches and kicks. We combine everything together. After black belt, we teach weapons like the nunchaku, bo and sai.

Would you describe your martial arts system and philosophy?

We begin by teaching the right attitude. The right attitude starts by treating students warmly to bring them into our school. I require my instructors to teach gently or go elsewhere. The military approach is important, but not for martial arts schools. A beginning student is much like a baby. They cannot walk, they cannot focus or punch correctly, so we have to teach them like a baby. Then slowly, after the first year, we help them develop tight discipline and tight attitude — tight and strong. By the time they reach black belt level they have developed the right attitude. Taekwondo mainly uses kicks, and I have dedicated most of my life to Korean styles they are what I know best. Personally, I love kicking and the art of taekwondo offers me a great variety of techniques in this particular aspect of combat. Hapkido is a great self-defense method and unintentionally I began to blend one system with the other in a natural way. Hapkido also emphasizes kicking, but in a different way. Kicking develops your legs, which in turn makes you a better fighter. If the legs are weak, it will be easy for your opponent to throw you off-balance. On the other hand, training the legs to kick makes them stronger — providing a good, solid stance.

As far as my philosophy goes, I would say that I believe in change — but change for the good and for a reason. The art of self-defense is not only for royal families or warriors. I teach a modern style, not because I made it that way but because that is the way taekwondo has evolved. As I said before, unintentionally and over a long period of time, I have blended hapkido and taekwondo techniques to create a number of self-defense combinations. These combinations happened naturally and I have been using and teaching them for years. By integrating elements from Japanese hand-techniques, I have made our punching more varied and complete. Also, traditional taekwondo never makes use of throws. Nevertheless I consider them very important for self-defense situations outside the ring. That's when hapkido comes in. A timely reverse punch, like those practiced in Japanese hard styles, are excellent for counterattacks or in combination with other techniques. As far as kicking, there is nothing like taekwondo. All I can say is that this system has proved very successful for tournament competition, and for the overall black belt quality of my students.

Do women need a different approach to train in the martial arts?

Just in the beginning. They need a little bit gentler training in the beginning, but after the first year, around blue belt, they are treated the same as the men. I like to teach women to have strong minds. I think nowadays, women have minds as strong as men. When it comes to dangerous moments, women have a stronger mind. I can appreciate women becoming black belts and not just honorary black belts. They must fight two against one, flip men around, perform jumping kicks, and break wood. I respect the more artistic way women do it. Men have more of a physical way behind their taekwonko. I like to encourage women in martial arts. They do very well. Sometimes when a women scores on a man, the man does not know what to do! He gets angry and loses his composure. This is stupid. When we become black belts, we choose to not let our feelings get out of control. Black belts learn to control their anger. If you are in a fight, never lose your mind. If you do that you can kill people or you can get killed. That is not the focus of martial arts.

How do you teach mind power?

There are many ways. Kiai, the yelling, is one. Also through breathing and sparring. Every one women, men and children must learn these things. If you've been sparring for four or five years, you become confident. After many years you have no fear at all of sparring. The same is true with jumping kicks. First the front-kick, then the side-kick followed by the back-kick, then double-kicks. Each time they master one method they get more confident and their mind becomes stronger. Step by step, they go through many obstacles. After a long and hard course, they become a black belt. Unfortunately, only one or two percent of the students get the black belt. I've been teaching for many years, but we only have over 200 black belts.

How often should a student train?

Three times a week is enough at first because the body needs time to recover especially from a hard taekwondo class. They cannot walk the next day after all the kicking. But once they are black belts they should train every day and stay with their martial arts. Many instructors become involved in movies, too. Once they get good, they take off and do movies. I've done many movies, but teaching always comes first and movies second. The school is always here. People come

to my school for how I teach because I teach sincerely. They might be drawn in because I've done movies, but that isn't right. They should come because of how we teach.

What is the essence of self-defense?

To me, self-defense is confidence and confidence comes from sparring. Taekwondo is a sparring art, and hapkido enables you to control your opponent. Thus, my students get a blend of the elements they need. If you spar a lot, a street fight should be very easy. If you don't spar, a street attack could be difficult because you won't even know how to relax your mind. Relaxation is the key element. In professional boxing, the first thing you learn is how to be calm so you can seize your chance. It's the same thing with the martial arts. You have to be calm so you can look for an opportunity to attack. It's the same thing in the street. You have to be calm. Wait for your chance. You don't want to panic. If you panic, you lose.

How important is discipline in your student's behavior?

I think it is the key to martial arts training. Without it, I don't think you'll find happiness. Discipline makes you better. When you are better, you are happy. If you are not happy with what you are doing, you will enjoy it less, train less, and be disappointed.

What does the future hold for you?

It's hard to tell. I would like to make more good martial arts movies. I'd like to stay away from too much fantasy. I'd prefer pure martial arts fighting scenes. I think realism is important. The movies with fantasy will come and go. After all these years, people still enjoy Enter the Dragon because it's more realistic than fantasy.

What would you like to say to all martial artists?

My advice is to stay interested and make martial arts a way of life. The martial arts way is a good one it contains discipline and confidence all of this can help you in your life. Many people start to train and then quit after a short time. Instead, make a long-term commitment. You must make a commitment or you will never be successful. Find what you like a good system and a good school and do long-term martial arts training. The rewards are there for you.

Jun Chong Martial Arts

Jun Chong Martial Arts

www.ingramcontent.com/pod-product-compliance
Lightning Source LLC
Chambersburg PA
CBHW040001080526
44586CB00027B/2837